# BULL RIDING

The ultimate guide in all you need
to know About Bull riding for
beginners

NANETTA BANANTO

# Table of Contents

# CHAPTER ONE

## INTRODUCTION

Bull riding is the maximum diagnosed as well as interesting rodeo sport wherein riders ought to keep their stability on a tamed bull for a selected duration of time. Considered as one of the most risky rodeo sports activities, in which injuries are an element and parcel of the sport, it requires flexibility, coordination, courage and high spirit to compete.

In this sport, the rider needs to mount at the bull for 8 seconds whilst keeping his stability on it, even as the bull constantly attempts to knock-off the rider at some stage in that period. If the rider successfully holds onto the bull for 8 seconds, he will get points primarily based on his driving competencies and the hurdles confronted at some point of the trip through a set of judges. The maximum scorer might be declared because the winner.

## Common bull using injuries

1.      Knee Ligament Injuries

2.      Shoulder Dislocation

3.      Ankle Sprains

4.      Contusions

5.      Concussions

1. Knee Ligament Injuries

Knee ligament injuries are particularly not unusual in the damaging world of bull using. Knee ligament injuries range from

Anterior Cruciate Ligament, Posterior Cruciate Ligament, Medial Collateral Ligament, and the Lateral Collateral Ligament. All of these ligaments surround the knee and join the shin bone to the thigh bone. These painful injuries are so not unusual because when bull riders are thrown off the bull, the force of whilst they're thrown off typically make the bull riders land incorrectly and tear those muscle tissue.

2. Shoulder Dislocation

Sustaining a dislocated shoulder on the rodeo is a not unusual prevalence. A shoulder dislocation is whilst the arm bone has been ejected from the shoulder socket. This damage is common due to the fact the objective of bull using is to maintain directly to the harness of the bull for as many seconds as viable, and the shoulder socket is strained while the bull will become excited and goals to throw the bull rider off its returned. The regular jerking of the bull takes a terrible effect on the shoulder, and has dislocated riders still mounted on the bull. When this occurs, bull riders want to get off the bull and right into a safe area with a view to are seeking medical attention.

## 3. Ankle Sprains

Ankle sprains are very commonplace in lots of sports activities and bull using isn't any exception. An ankle sprain is while the tendons and ligaments that surround the ankle are stretched or torn, inflicting the ankle to emit a popping sound as well as start to swell and feature a dark bruise form within the affected vicinity. Bull riders often sustain ankle sprains when they're thrown off the bull and land awkwardly at the ankle, commonly by rolling it. This is a extra serious injury than in different sports due to the fact bull riders should run out of the bullpen as rapid as possible and climb over the metal fence, and having an ankle sprain makes running lots greater difficult.

## 4. Contusions

Getting a contusion inside the bullpen is almost 2nd nature to bull riders. A contusion is the medically correct terminology for a bruise, and it's far whilst direct stress is in opposition to the pores and skin, causing ache and having the blood capillaries leak, generating the typical black-and-blue. For bull riders, contusions are part of the game; many bull riders get contusions from being attacked by means of the bull and through hitting the steel fence so speedy and so hard strolling far from the excited bull. A contusion isn't always a totally critical damage with the aid of nature, but whilst the injury is due to a big animal, many bull riders choose scientific attention.

## 5. Concussions

In this type of dangerous game, it is not unusual for a bull rider to be concussed on the rodeo. A concussion is a severe head injury, inflicting transient reminiscence loss, issue in awareness, and brief balance impairments. This harm can be resulting from an unexpected and direct blow to the head. Every time a bull rider sits at the lower back of a bull, they may be aware of the possible implications of being thrown off the bull and touchdown at the flat dirt on their head, or maybe worse, being hit by means of the bull within the head. Bull riders ought to be searching for immediately clinical attention if this takes place on the rodeo.

# CHAPTER TWO

## Bull Riding Equipment

Bull rider's use quite some gadget's intended for his or her protection to keep away from accidents and most protection for them and for the animal concerned. The distinctive styles of device utilized by a rider are defined within the following subheads.

Bull Rope – the bull rope is taken into consideration because the number one gadget in bull using. It is more often than not tied around the bull's girth location at the back of its front legs. It is in the main made from Nylon, grass and a mixture of some different materials. A take care of is braided at the centre of the rope which is similarly stiffened by means of leather.

The facet of the rope this is tied to the bull is tied in an adjustable knot in an effort to permit adjustment primarily based at the bull's length. The other facet of the rope has a flat braid and is lined with rosin which permits the rope to keep on sliding from the rider's hand to be able to avoid accidents.

The deal with is partially made from leather and is the only assist for the rider all through the experience. A bell is strapped to the knot which lets in the rope to fall of the bull once the rider has been dismounted from the bull.

Chaps – Chaps are the maximum visible component among the rider's entire gadget. They are more often than not product of leather-based and regularly printed with the sponsor's call. They can also appearance ornamental and flashy, but they are part of the rider's armour and offer protection for the rider's thigh and leg components in opposition to the bull's horns and hooves.

Gloves – Riders use simplest one glove at the hand that's used to grip the rope during the experience. These gloves are in particular made of leather and are used to save you rope burns and offer protection to the palms and hands. The gloves also are used as a good grip over the rope. Some riders use rosin at the gloves which permits additional grip over the rope

Cowboy hats and helmets – the flashiest and most distinguished a part of a bull rider's gadget is the cowboy hat. It is in general used that allows you to offer safety from head injuries and maintaining the balance. Now days some riders are the usage of helmets and defensive masks for additional safety.

Some expert riders nonetheless decide upon cowboy hats over helmets as they believe that the helmet impacts their stability for the duration of the ride. While the helmet offers additional protection to a few susceptible components of head, the face masks is basically used for supplying safety to stand and jaw regions.

Boots – the cowboy boots are especially designed for bull riding. They have a unique spur ridge at the hill which allows the spurs live on the area. The loosely locked spurs are used to keep stability for the duration of the journey and are considered as one of the most crucial system.

Protective vests – The shielding vests used by the bull riders prevents blow to the frame and protects the rider's torso part against the direct touch with the bull's horn and hooves component. Only PBR bull riders use these vests for added safety.

# Bull Equipment

Flank strap – A flank strap is a rope that is manufactured from soft cotton of around 5 to 8 inches in dimension and is tied to the bull's flank place. Contrary to the rumours, a flank strap isn't always tied to the bull's testicles. It is ordinarily used to encourage the bull to apply its hind legs extra in the course of bucking.

As the bulls are very ticklish on the flank area, tying the flank strap permits them to buck greater without any injury. If the flank strap is tied improperly, a rider can apply for a re trip because the bull doesn't greenback properly if the flank strap is simply too tight. The flank strap is frequently tied with the aid of a stock contractor or his designates.

## Bull Riding - Playing Environment

The arenas which can be used for bull using vary from every other. Some arenas are constructed only for bull riding and different rodeo sports activities, whilst others are used to play other games except bull riding. The length of this area in the main relies upon on the typical venue. Mostly it's far a massive region which gives the rider in addition to the bull enough area to manoeuvre.

At one cease of the area, bucking chutes are there from which the bulls are launched. These chutes are small square formed places wherein the rider also mounts at the bull at the start and the bull rushes into the area with the rider established on it. Another go out chute is there thru which the bulls can go out the arena.

# Bull Riding - Rules

In bull riding, there aren't many disqualification regulations. Rules are set round the sport method as well as scorings. Different corporations follow specific set of policies and different occasion organizing strategies. Even the minimum ride time differs from one organization to some other.

Many of the bull riding competitions contain multiple rounds and spans over to three nights. A rider is permitted to experience most effective one bull in one night time. The total factors at the end of the occasion are recorded. Mostly after rounds, primarily based on the overall factors scored by means of the riders for the primary two days, pinnacle 20 gamers are selected.

Among the ones top 20 players, every other round of competition is prepared among them. The final spherical is known as Short Go on the quit of whom the best scorer wins the opposition.

The rider makes use of spurs to inspire the bull to perform extra moves. Modern rodeo policies are very strict approximately the usage of the spurs. These spurs utilized in competitions can neither have a hard and fast rowel nor can they be sharpened. PBR simplest allows the usage of varieties of spurs to make sure the safety of the animal.

If a rider scores low due to the bull's low overall performance, he can appeal for a re-experience. The judges allow a loose re-journey to the rider only if they feel that the bull didn't deliver its exceptional or underperformed as compared to other bulls of the occasion. The judges signal the re-journey by way of throwing a pink flag into the area.

By taking up the re-trip option, the rider has to surrender the scores received and wait until other riders end off their trip and then he rides again. Sometimes the plan backfires whilst the rider receives low in the first journey, however gets zero or lower score within the 2nd experience. A rider is likewise given a re-journey if the bull both stumbles or runs off to the gate.

If the chute countdown time expires before the rider offers his nod, either the bull or the rider gets disqualified via the judges based totally on the situation. If the bull gets disqualified, the rider gets a re-experience, whereas if a rider receives disqualified the trip gets over.

# CHAPTER THREE

# BULL RIDING - HOW TO RIDE

In this bankruptcy, we are able to get to realize the way to mount a bull, to ride and about the fundamental protection measures of driving.

## Riding Basics

Riders and bulls are commonly matched up randomly before the start of the healthy itself. However, in some cases, ranked riders are allowed to select the bull for driving. Each bull has a particular call and variety and is chosen based totally on its energy, health, agility, age and so on.

## Mounting the Bull

First the rider mounts the bull and grips the flat braided rope. Once he has secured an amazing grip at the rope, he nods which indicates he is ready and the sport begins. The area is fenced up to 6 to 7 ft high for you to shield the audience from the escaped bulls.

## Exits

Generally, exits are there at each corner of the arena which lets in the riders to get out of the way right away. Sometimes, in case of emergency, riders also can hop directly to the fence to avoid hazard. The bucking chute (a small enclosure in which the bull is held) will be open and the bull will storm in to the area.

## Race

The minimal riding time for qualification is 8 seconds in keeping with American guidelines. The clock starts off evolved as soon as the bull breaks the aircraft of the gate. The rider wishes to live on the bull for the complete time whilst touching the bull the usage of only his using hand. The other hand of the rider is loose for the relaxation of the race.

During the race, the bull attempts each manner to throw off the rider from itself by bucking, jumping, kicking, spinning or twisting itself while the rider wishes to live at the bull for 8 seconds. In case of bareback using and saddle bronc, the riders can't use their free hand to touch the bull as this will result in stop of the ride.

The riders normally use rosin, that's a sticky substance, with a view to have a firm grip over the rope throughout the using length. The riders use their weight for shifting over the bucking bull during the trip time for you to keep the bull.

The journey time ends if –

•    The rider's hand comes out of the rope.

•    The rider touches the ground.

•    The loose hand of the rider touches the bull (also referred to as slap).

A buzzer or whistle pronounces the finishing touch of the 8-second ride.

Throughout the game, bull fighters, additionally known as rodeo clowns, stay near the bull in an effort to help the rider each time wished. Sometime for the duration of time of emergency, the rider can also leap off the fence to break out from the bull while the rodeo clowns attempt to distract the bull.

**Scoring**

In case of bull driving, the winner is said based totally on the judge's rating. Both the rider and the bull are presented rankings. Usually there are two judges for the sport and each judge presents rankings to the bull from 0 to 50 factors and to the rider from zero to 50.

The combined rating from every choose is considered because the final rating for the rider. Sometimes gamers score zero points that are pretty common in the case wherein the rider straight away falls off from the bull after leaving the chute itself. Many skilled specialists generally rating greater than 75.

The score above eighty is considered high-quality, above 90 is outstanding and really rare. It's nearly impossible for a participant to score complete factors i.E. One hundred. Till now, in the records of bull riding, it only happened as soon as in which a rider has been given complete a hundred points.

The ratings given by the judges are based totally on many elements. A rider receives rating based totally on his potential to govern in addition to consistency at the same time as mounting at the bull. A rider is only provided score, if he has stayed on for more than eight seconds at the bull. Sometimes while at the bull, the riders carry out spurring if you want to gain extra points. The rider receives disqualified if he touches the bull or the rope or himself using his free arm. The ability to manipulate the bull offers the rider extra greater factors.

The bulls utilized in the sport have raw energy and distinctive movement styles compared to different rodeo game animals.

Sometimes they carry out sunfishing or stomach roll, wherein the bull jumps and whilst being absolutely off the floor, the bull kicks his hind facet in a twisting or rolling movement which makes it really tough for the rider to keep onto the bull.

The bull continually gets a rating despite the fact that the rider falls off from it inside 8 seconds. For the bull, the judges see its pace, agility and the diploma of difficulty it is placing for the rider. Judges specially search for it's the front give up drops, lower back end kicks, spins and route modifications. If a bull offers the rider a absolutely hard time, more rankings are provided to it.

Based on the beyond document factors of the bulls, satisfactory bulls are delivered to the final fits so that you can make certain superb competition and proper score to the riders. Good scores provide "Bucking Bull of the Year" award to the bull, which brings prestige to the particular bull's ranch.

# CHAPTER FOUR

# BULL RIDING

Bull riding is the maximum identified in addition to thrilling rodeo recreation in which riders should hold their balance on a tamed bull for a particular length of time. Considered as one of the most risky rodeo sports activities, in which injuries are a part and parcel of the sport, it calls for flexibility, coordination, braveness and excessive spirit to compete.

In this recreation, the rider wishes to mount on the bull for 8 seconds at the same time as maintaining his balance on it, while the bull constantly tries to knock-off the rider at some point of that length. If the rider efficiently holds onto the bull for 8 seconds, he's going to get factors primarily based on his driving competencies and the hurdles confronted throughout the ride by way of a set of judges. The maximum scorer might be declared because the winner.

Common bull using accidents?

1.      Knee Ligament Injuries

2.      Shoulder Dislocation

3.      Ankle Sprains

4.      Contusions

5.      Concussions

1. Knee Ligament Injuries

Knee ligament injuries are pretty common in the harmful global of bull driving. Knee ligament injuries range from Anterior Cruciate

Ligament, Posterior Cruciate Ligament, Medial Collateral Ligament, and the Lateral Collateral Ligament. All of these ligaments surround the knee and join the shin bone to the thigh bone. These painful accidents are so common because when bull riders are thrown off the bull, the pressure of when they may be thrown off commonly make the bull riders land incorrectly and tear the ones muscle mass.

## 2. Shoulder Dislocation

Sustaining a dislocated shoulder on the rodeo is a commonplace occurrence. A shoulder dislocation is whilst the arm bone has been ejected from the shoulder socket. This damage is not unusual because the goal of bull riding is to maintain on to the harness of the bull for as many seconds as possible, and the shoulder socket is strained whilst the bull turns into excited and objectives to throw the bull rider off its returned. The consistent jerking of the bull takes a terrible impact on the shoulder, and has dislocated riders still hooked up at the bull. When this happens, bull riders want to get off the bull and right into a secure area with a purpose to searching for medical interest.

## 3. Ankle Sprains

Ankle sprains are very common in many sports and bull riding is no exception. An ankle sprain is while the tendons and ligaments that surround the ankle are stretched or torn, causing the ankle to emit a popping sound as well as start to swell and feature a darkish bruise form inside the affected area. Bull riders frequently sustain ankle sprains when they are thrown off the bull and land awkwardly on the ankle, generally via rolling it. This is a greater critical harm than in different sports because bull riders need to run out of the bullpen as rapid as feasible and climb over the metallic fence, and having an ankle sprain makes running a great deal greater tough.

4. Contusions

Getting a contusion in the bullpen is nearly second nature to bull riders. A contusion is the medically accurate terminology for a bruise, and it's far whilst direct stress is towards the skin, inflicting ache and having the blood capillaries leak, generating the standard black-and-blue. For bull riders, contusions are part of the sport; many bull riders get contusions from being attacked via the bull and through hitting the metallic fence so fast and so difficult running away from the excited bull. A contusion isn't always a totally extreme injury via nature, however whilst the damage is because of a large animal, many bull riders opt for scientific interest.

## 5. Concussions

In such a dangerous sport, it isn't always unusual for a bull rider to be concussed at the rodeo. A concussion is serious head harm, inflicting transient memory loss, difficulty in concentration, and brief stability impairments. This harm can be resulting from a surprising and direct blow to the pinnacle. Every time a bull rider sits on the returned of a bull, they're aware of the possible implications of being thrown off the bull and landing at the flat dirt on their head, or maybe worse, being hit by using the bull in the head. Bull riders need to seek immediate clinical interest if this occurs on the rodeo.

# Bull Riding Equipment

Bull rider's use pretty a few devices's meant for his or her safety to keep away from accidents and maximum protection for them and for the animal worried. The one-of-a-kind sorts of system utilized by a rider are explained inside the following subheads.

Bull Rope – the bull rope is considered because the primary gadget in bull using. It is in general tied around the bull's girth vicinity in the back of it's the front legs. It is frequently made from Nylon, grass and a combination of a few other substances. A cope with is braided at the centre of the rope which is in addition stiffened by means of leather-based.

The facet of the rope this is tied to the bull is tied in an adjustable knot if you want to allow adjustment based on the bull's size. The different facet of the rope has a flat braid and is coated with rosin which allows the rope to keep on sliding from the rider's hand for you to avoid injuries.

The deal with is partly made of leather-based and is the simplest guide for the rider in the course of the journey. A bell is strapped to the knot which permits the rope to fall of the bull as soon as the rider has been dismounted from the bull.

Chaps – Chaps are the most seen component among the rider's entire gadget. They are often manufactured from leather and often published with the sponsor's call. They may additionally look ornamental and flashy, but they're a part of the rider's armour and provide safety for the rider's thigh and leg parts against the bull's horns and hooves.

Gloves – Riders use simplest one glove on the hand which is used to grip the rope for the duration of the journey. These gloves are especially fabricated from leather-based and are used to prevent rope burns and provide safety to the arms and hands. The gloves also are used as a great grip over the rope. Some riders use rosin on the gloves which permits additional grip over the rope

Cowboy hats and helmets – the flashiest and maximum distinguished a part of a bull rider's equipment is the cowboy hat. It is commonly used so that it will offer safety from head accidents and preserving the balance. Now a daze a few riders are the use of helmets and protective mask for extra safety.

Some professional riders still decide on cowboy hats over helmets as they trust that the helmet impacts their stability all through the trip. While the helmet gives extra protection to a few vulnerable elements of head, the face masks is normally used for imparting safety to stand and jaw regions.

Boots – the cowboy boots are specially designed for bull riding. They have a special spur ridge on the hill which allows the spurs stay on the area. The loosely locked spurs are used to keep stability at some point of the trip and are taken into consideration as one of the maximum critical device.

Protective vests – The shielding vests used by the bull riders prevents blow to the body and protects the rider's torso part towards the direct touch with the bull's horn and hooves element. Only PBR bull riders use these vests for added safety.

# BULL EQUIPMENT

Flank strap – A flank strap is a rope that is made from soft cotton of round 5 to 8 inches in dimension and is tied to the bull's flank area. Contrary to the rumours, a flank strap isn't always tied to the bull's testicles. It is primarily used to encourage the bull to use its hind legs more at some stage in bucking.

As the bulls are very ticklish on the flank place, tying the flank strap enables them to dollar greater with none damage. If the flank strap is tied improperly, a rider can practice for a re trip as the bull doesn't buck well if the flank strap is just too tight. The flank strap is frequently tied by means of an inventory contractor or his designates.

## Bull Riding - Playing Environment

The arenas that are used for bull riding vary from each different. Some arenas are constructed best for bull using and other rodeo sports, while others are used to play different video games except bull driving. The size of this area normally relies upon on the typical venue. Mostly it's far a huge area which offers the rider in addition to the bull enough space to manoeuvre.

At one quit of the arena, bucking chutes are there from which the bulls are released. These chutes are small rectangular formed locations where the rider also mounts at the bull at the start and the bull rushes into the arena with the rider hooked up on it. Another go out chute is there via which the bulls can go out the arena.

## Bull Riding - Rules

In bull riding, there aren't many disqualification regulations. Rules are set around the game method in addition to scorings. Different agencies follow extraordinary set of guidelines and extraordinary event organizing techniques. Even the minimum experience time differs from one enterprise to some other.

Many of the bull driving competitions involve more than one round and spans over to a few nights. A rider is allowed to journey handiest one bull in one night time. The overall factors at the give up of the event are recorded. Mostly after rounds, primarily based on the overall factors scored through the riders for the first days, top 20 players are decided on.

Among those pinnacle 20 gamers, any other spherical of opposition is organized amongst them. The final spherical is known as Short Go on the give up of which the highest scorer wins the competition.

The rider uses spurs to inspire the bull to perform more movements. Modern rodeo rules are very strict about the usage of the spurs. These spurs used in competitions can neither have a set rowel nor can they be sharpened. PBR best lets in the usage of two styles of spurs to ensure the protection of the animal.

If a rider rankings low due to the bull's low overall performance, he cans enchantment for a re-ride. The judges permit a free re-experience to the rider most effective in the event that they experience that the bull didn't give its great or underperformed as compared to different bulls of the occasion. The judges sign the re-trip by way of throwing a red flag into the arena.

By taking over the re-experience alternative, the rider has to give up the ratings received and wait until different riders finish off their experience after which he rides again. Sometimes the plan backfires when the rider receives low inside the first journey, however receives zero or lower score in the 2d experience. A rider is also given a re-ride if the bull both stumbles or runs off to the gate.

If the chute countdown time expires earlier than the rider offers his nod, both the bull and the rider receives disqualified via the judges based at the state of affairs. If the bull gets disqualified, the rider receives a re-trip, while if a rider gets disqualified the journey receives over.

# Riding Basics

Riders and bulls are normally matched up randomly before the start of the healthy itself. However, in some cases, ranked riders are allowed to pick out the bull for using. Each bull has a particular name and quantity and is chosen based on its electricity, fitness, agility, age and so forth.

## Mounting the Bull

First the rider mounts the bull and grips the flat braided rope. Once he has secured an amazing grip at the rope, he nods which indicates he is ready and the sport starts. The area is fenced up to 6 to 7 toes high if you want to guard the target audience from the escaped bulls.

## Exits

Generally, exits are there at every corner of the area which permits the riders to get out of the manner right away. Sometimes, in case of emergency, riders can also hop directly to the fence to keep away from chance. The bucking chute (a small enclosure where the bull is held) could be open and the bull will typhoon in to the area.

## Race

The minimal riding time for qualification is eight seconds according to American guidelines. The clock begins once the bull breaks the plane of the gate. The rider desires to stay at the bull for the complete time at the same time as touching the bull using simplest his using hand. The other hand of the rider is free for the rest of the race.

During the race, the bull attempts each manner to throw off the rider from itself via bucking, jumping, kicking, spinning or twisting itself whereas the rider needs to stay at the bull for eight seconds. In case of bareback driving and saddle bronc, the riders can't use their unfastened hand to the touch the bull as this could result in end of the journey.

The riders commonly use rosin, which is a sticky substance, on the way to have a company grip over the rope during the using duration. The riders use their weight for transferring over the bucking bull during the trip time so that it will hold the bull.

The journey time ends if –

- The rider's hand comes out of the rope.

- The rider touches the floor.

- The free hand of the rider touches the bull (also referred to as slap).

A buzzer or whistle publicizes the completion of the eight-2nd experience.

Throughout the game, bull combatants, also referred to as rodeo clowns, live close to the bull on the way to assist the rider every time wanted. Sometime during time of emergency, the rider can also leap off the fence to escape from the bull while the rodeo clowns try to distract the bull.

**Scoring**

In case of bull driving, the winner is declared based totally on the judge's rating. Both the rider and the bull are offered ratings. Usually there are judges for the sport and every decide affords ratings to the bull from zero to 50 points and to the rider from 0 to 50.

The blended score from each choose is taken into consideration because the final rating for the rider. Sometimes gamers rating zero points that are quite common within the case wherein the rider at once falls off from the bull after leaving the chute itself. Many skilled specialists normally rating more than seventy five.

The score above 80 is considered fantastic, above 90 is extremely good and very rare. It's almost impossible for a participant to score complete points i.E. 100. Till now, inside the records of bull riding, it most effective passed off once in which a rider has been given full a hundred factors.

The ratings given by the judges are based on many elements. A rider gets rating based on his ability to manipulate in addition to consistency whilst mounting at the bull. A rider is simplest presented score, if he has stayed on for extra than eight seconds at the bull. Sometimes even as on the bull, the riders perform spurring to be able to benefit extra factors. The rider receives disqualified if he touches the bull or the rope or himself the usage of his free arm. The ability to manipulate the bull affords the rider extra factors.

The bulls used in the game have raw energy and distinct motion patterns compared to other rodeo sport animals. Sometimes they perform sunfishing or stomach roll, wherein the bull jumps and at the same time as being absolutely off the floor, the bull kicks his hind facet in a twisting or rolling motion which makes it simply tough for the rider to preserve onto the bull.

The bull always gets a score even though the rider falls off from it inside eight seconds. For the bull, the judges see its velocity, agility and the diploma of problem it's far setting for the rider. Judges particularly search for it's the front quit drops, lower back cease kicks, spins and path changes. If a bull offers the rider a truly difficult time, extra scores are awarded to it.

Based on the beyond report points of the bulls, first-class bulls are added to the very last fits in order to ensure exceptional opposition and exact rating to the riders. Good rankings offer "Bucking Bull of the Year" award to the bull, which brings prestige to the particular bull's ranch.

THE END

www.ingramcontent.com/pod-product-compliance
Lightning Source LLC
Chambersburg PA
CBHW060810260726
48660CB00002B/870

# WALL PILATES FOR WOMEN OVER 60

Step-by-step illustrated low impact exercise to improve mobility and regain flexibility.

By Desmond T. Hall

# Copyright © 2024 by Desmond T. Hall



## Declaimer ⚠️

This book is a work of nonfiction. Names, characters, places, and incidents are either the product of the author's imagination or are used fictitiously. Any resemblance to actual persons, living or dead, business establishments, events, or locales is entirely coincidental.

## OTHER BOOKS BY THIS AUTHOR

### Scan the QR Code Below to Get Access